Dear Diary; I've Committed a Capital Offense

Dear Diary Style Files, Volume 4

Saoirse Temple

Published by Saoirse Temple, 2025.

While every precaution has been taken in the preparation of this book, the publisher assumes no responsibility for errors or omissions, or for damages resulting from the use of the information contained herein.

DEAR DIARY; I'VE COMMITTED A CAPITAL OFFENSE

First edition. September 8, 2025.

Copyright © 2025 Saoirse Temple.

ISBN: 978-1069750518

Written by Saoirse Temple.

Table of Contents

An Uppercase Uprising 1
Entry 1: Capital Punishment 3
Entry 2: The "I" Problem 5
Entry 3: Title Tantrums 7
Entry 4: Royal Pains 9
Entry 5: Brand Ego Trips 11
Entry 6: Geography Gone Wild 13
Entry 7: Seasonal Affective Capitalization Disorder 15
Entry 8: Days of Our Lives 17
Entry 9: Holy Caps, Batman! 20
Entry 10: Acronym Drama 23
Entry 11: The Capital of Creativity 26
Entry 12: Family Feud 28
Entry 13: Academic Inflations 30
Capital Crimes Report 32
Glossary of Capital Confusion 34
It's Time to Play... Cap or No Cap? 37
Cap or No Cap? Answer Key 40
A Sneak Peek at What's to Come 41

For Vicky

An Uppercase Uprising

Dear Diary,

    I have committed a capital offense. Literally. Everywhere I turn, capital letters are bossing me around—at the beginning of sentences, strutting around in names, shouting from headlines, and sometimes popping up where they don't belong just to make me look foolish. Lowercase letters are calm, steady, and unassuming. Capitals, though? They're the extroverts of the alphabet. They arrive overdressed, hog the spotlight, and insist on being noticed.

    Take the start of a sentence. That first capital isn't optional; it's mandatory, like showing your ID before you buy wine. Forget it, and suddenly your sentence looks naked, embarrassed, and a little cold. *"this is how it feels without a capital."* See? Like I've turned up to a job interview wearing slippers. Capital letters know they're indispensable, and they never let us forget it.

    And then there's **I**. The one pronoun that insists on standing tall no matter where it goes. Why does "I" get a capital when "you," "he," and "she" are left slouching? It's pure ego. A lonely vertical line strutting around like it owns the joint. If letters had social media, "I" would definitely be an influencer.

    Proper nouns, of course, are obsessed with their capitals. Cities, rivers, landmarks—they all preen like they're in a yearbook photo. "Look at me," says the **Mississippi River**. "I'm not just any river. I'm *The* River." And then you have brand names—**Coca-Cola**, **Nike**, **McDonald's**—parading around like neon signs, while poor generic cola has to shuffle along in lowercase shame.

    But capitals don't always know when to leave the party. Random Words sometimes show up in the Middle of a Sentence, capitalized for No Reason at All, like they've had too much champagne. You see this in business memos, government notices, and anywhere someone wants to

Look Official. It doesn't fool anyone, Diary. It just makes the sentence look like it tripped over its own shoes.

And then there is this: **ALL CAPS!** Basically ALL CAPS is the drunk uncle at Thanksgiving. Sometimes it's useful for headlines or acronyms, but more often it's just yelling at me from across the internet. *"BUY NOW! LIMITED TIME ONLY!"* Yes, thank you, I'll pass. Lowercase may be soft-spoken, but at least it doesn't give me a headache.

It doesn't help that every style guide has a different opinion on capitalization. Chicago Manual of Style (CMoS) says one thing, AP says another, MLA whispers from the corner like a shy cousin, and tech companies just make up their own rules as they go. It's less a rulebook and more a Choose Your Own Adventure. Do you capitalize "internet"? Depends on what year it is. Do you capitalize job titles? Ask three editors and get four answers.

Still, Diary, I have to admit: capitals aren't all bad. Sometimes they really do pull their weight. Take "Polish" vs. "polish." One is a person from Warsaw, the other is what I put on my nails when I'm procrastinating. Case closed. And there's something satisfying about a perfectly balanced Title Case headline, or a reverent capital letter used sparingly for emphasis. Capitals can elevate. They can inspire. They just need to stop acting like every sentence is their runway.

So here I am, working through my love–hate relationship with these alphabet divas. I'll complain, I'll confess, I'll probably capitalize something I shouldn't and have to apologize for it later. But maybe—just maybe—I'll figure out how to keep my Capitals in line.

Yours Uprisingly,
The Writer Stirring Up Trouble in Uppercase

Entry 1: Capital Punishment

Dear Diary,

I am writing this from a prison of my own making. My crime? Forgetting to capitalize the first word of a sentence. The sentence looked so small and harmless at the time, sitting there with its lowercase letter at the front like a toddler trying on its mother's shoes. I thought I could get away with it. But the Grammar Police saw it instantly, and now I'm serving time.

It seems harsh, doesn't it? To be sentenced over a single shift key slip. And yet that's the weight of capitalization. One missing capital, and suddenly it looks like I don't know how sentences work. One forgotten "M" in "Monday," and the world thinks I'm writing ransom notes. One lowercase "i," and I've apparently joined the secret society of internet poets who believe capital letters are tools of oppression.

I've been charged before. I once sent an email without capitalizing someone's name. Oh, the fallout. You'd have thought I'd keyed their car or insulted their grandmother. Nothing makes a reader clutch their pearls faster than seeing their own name dressed in lowercase. It's like showing up to a royal banquet in ripped jeans. A capital letter is more than a courtesy — it's armor plating for the ego.

The sentencing is always the same. A teacher's red pen. An editor's raised eyebrow. A friend's passive-aggressive text pointing out that "Canada is a country, you know." No appeals, no second chances. Just the swift, merciless smack of capital punishment.

I can't help but notice how smug capitals are about this power. The capital "T" doesn't just begin a sentence — it presides over it like a judge in robes. A capital "W" doesn't stroll in quietly; it slams the gavel, demanding order. Even the humble capital "L" seems to leer at me, as if daring me to slip and write *london* instead of *London*. They're waiting for me to mess up, so they can add another charge to my record.

A teacher once told me that the capital letter at the beginning of a sentence is more than just a tall piece of type—it's punctuation in disguise. It acts like a second stop sign. The period ends the old thought, and the capital shouts: "New thought starts here!" Maybe that's why my lowercase experiments feel so strange. Without the capital, my sentence has no trumpet to announce its arrival.

But here's the real torment, Diary: I know I'm guilty, and I'll do it again. My typing is fast, my attention span is short, and the shift key is a fraction of an inch farther away than I want it to be. One moment of laziness and the damage is done. The capital is missing. The punishment is swift. The shame is eternal.

And yet, despite the fear of imprisonment, I have to admit there's something thrilling about capital letters. They're not just rules; they're drama. A lowercase "turkey" is dinner; a capital "Turkey" is a country. A lowercase "march" is a slow parade down the street; a capital "March" is a whole month of my life gone in a blur. Capitals aren't just letters—they're verdicts.

So yes, I'll keep obeying. I'll serve my sentence faithfully. Because if I don't, my writing turns into a crime scene, and the Grammar Police don't take bribes. At least not the ones armed with red pens.

Yours guiltily,
The Writer Who Serves Her Sentence Willingly

Entry 2: The "I" Problem

Dear Diary,

There's only one pronoun in English that insists on being capitalized every single time. Not "he," not "she," not even "we." Just plain old "I."

And doesn't that say it all?

"I" is the Beyoncé of pronouns—the one-letter diva demanding the spotlight. In lowercase, it's just a scrawny little stick with a dot, barely noticeable. Maybe that's why it insists on standing tall.

So up it goes, strutting through sentences like a flagpole in designer heels. While every other pronoun blends humbly into the crowd, "I" plants itself front and center.

Imagine if the other pronouns behaved this way. If "she" were "She," Aunt Gertrude would look like royalty. If "they" were "They," essays would read like cult manifestos. But no — only "I" gets this privilege. The rest toil away in lowercase while "I" demands the shift key every single time.

No one really knows who to blame. Some medieval monk, probably, squinting by candlelight, decided the little stick figure of "i" looked too pitiful and said, *"This one's special—let's supersize it."* Instead of laughing him back to blotter duty, everyone agreed. Centuries later, I'm still tapping the shift key, indulging the ego of a single letter.

And the worst part? It works. Write "i" in lowercase and it looks timid, apologetic, like it needs reassurance. Capital "I" stands straighter, louder, more assured—and maybe a little smug.

People notice. Text someone "i'm fine," and it sounds like a cry for help. Text "I'M FINE," and sure, it's still a lie, but at least it's confident.

It's unfair, really. In French, "je" toddles along in lowercase without complaint. In Spanish, "yo" stays modest. Only English gives one pronoun this kind of special treatment. If pronouns were siblings, "I" would be the spoiled youngest child, getting cake for dinner while the others eat their vegetables.

And yet, I keep enabling it. Every time I hit that shift key, I reinforce its belief that the page revolves around it. Without me, it would shrink back to a shy little stick with a dot. But no, I dress it up in capital couture, and it struts across the page like it owns the sentence.

Maybe that's the trick, though. Maybe "I" isn't just a diva. Maybe it's a confidence booster cleverly disguised as a pronoun. Lowercase "i" feels small and timid. Capital "I" declares: *I exist. I matter. I will not be ignored.*

Yours reluctantly,
The Writer Who Keeps Feeding "I"'s Ego

Entry 3: Title Tantrums

Dear Diary,

Today I got into a fight with capitalization over job titles. Not with real people—though I've managed to offend a few of those too—but with the words themselves. Titles are greedy. They want capital letters the way toddlers want candy: all the time, and preferably in excess.

Take "manager." In lowercase, it's a perfectly reasonable word. Someone who manages things. But stick it in front of a name—"Manager Bob"—and suddenly the M inflates like an entitled Gen-Xer. That's the rule: when a job title appears *directly before* a person's name, it gets a capital. *President Lincoln. Doctor Watson. Assistant Manager of Coffee Distribution Bob.* The moment that title wanders off on its own, though, it loses its capital privileges. *Lincoln was the president. Watson was a doctor. Bob was still just the assistant manager of coffee.* It's like a child star who looks glamorous on stage but has to take out the trash like every other kid when they get home.

And yet, so many people sprinkle capitals on titles wherever they appear, as if "Director" and "Supervisor" are holy words. I once saw an email signature that read "Director Of Operations At The Regional Office." Every Word A Monument. It looked less like a job description and more like a carved inscription on a tombstone.

Book and movie titles throw their own tantrums. *Title Case* is supposed to make them look important, but mostly it makes me look indecisive. Which words do I capitalize? Nouns, verbs, adjectives, sure—but what about little guys like "of," "to," or "with"? Some style guides say keep them lowercase. Others insist you only capitalize words if they're longer than four letters. It's like playing Whack-A-Mole with words. Just when I think I've nailed it, "About" pops up demanding its own capital crown.

Then there's sentence case — the more casual cousin. Here, you capitalize only the first word and any proper nouns, just like in an ordinary sentence. So instead of *The Cat Who Came To Dinner*, you'd have *The cat who came to dinner*. It looks relaxed, approachable, maybe even modern. But sentence case titles can also look like the typesetter nodded off mid-shift. Still, there's a case to be made for sentence case: it shines in subtitles. *Writer Masters Capitalization: She's got this!*

Of course, all of this is before we get to the real headline monsters: ALL CAPS. I once read a news headline written entirely in capitals and panicked. I thought the building was on fire. No, it was just a city council meeting. But the words were screaming at me as though I needed to evacuate.

The truth is, titles are insecure creatures. Sentences have punctuation to tell you where they begin and end, but titles are out there naked, with nothing but whitespace to define them. Capitals swoop in like flashy bodyguards, making sure everyone notices. And the words eat it up. "Look at me! I'm a Title! Don't you dare try to lowercase me!"

Sometimes I imagine stripping them down to all lowercase — *war and peace, pride and prejudice, the lord of the rings*. Chic, minimalist, the kind of thing you'd find in a trendy bookstore where the staff wear ironic glasses and sigh loudly when you ask where the bathroom is. But deep down, I know I'll keep obeying the rules. I'll capitalize "President Lincoln" but not "the president." I'll wrestle with "in" and "on" until one of us cries. And I'll sigh when I see "Director Of My Own Destiny" proudly plastered across someone's LinkedIn page.

Yours inconsistently,
The Writer Who Keeps Bowing To Title Tantrums

Entry 4: Royal Pains

Dear Diary,

I have discovered that monarchs and other Very Important People are basically toddlers in crowns. The proof? They throw tantrums if you don't capitalize their titles.

It's true. Put "Queen Elizabeth" on the page and everything looks proper, regal, steeped in centuries of tradition. Drop the capital and write "queen Elizabeth," and suddenly she sounds like someone's Aunt Liz who brings a casserole to the church potluck. Same woman, different wardrobe. That single capital letter is the royal cloak; without it, she's just standing in line at the grocery store staring at the tabloid headlines.

And it's not just queens. Presidents, popes, prime ministers—all of them insist on capital treatment when their title comes before their name. *President Lincoln. Pope Francis. Prime Minister Trudeau.* The moment you slide the title behind the name, though, the capital vanishes like a servant ducking out of sight. *Lincoln was the president. Francis is the pope. Trudeau is the prime minister.* See? They're still important, but they've been politely shoved back into lowercase, as if the spotlight moved on.

It's a delicate balance. Too many capitals, and your writing looks like it's been bedazzled by an overzealous court jester. Too few, and you risk looking disrespectful—or worse, like you don't know the rules. No one wants to be accused of treason by their copyeditor.

And then there are the gray areas. Should "royal highness" be capitalized every time, or only when you're addressing the person directly? Does "the crown" get a capital when it refers to the institution, or only when it's sitting on someone's actual head? These are the sorts of questions that keep writers up at night while the rest of the world peacefully binges television.

Of course, the irony is that royalty doesn't exist in everyone's daily lives anymore, but the capitalization rules cling like ivy on a castle wall.

We treat "King Charles" with reverence on the page, even if half of us couldn't care less about his breakfast routine. Capitals don't ask whether you like the person—they simply insist you acknowledge the throne they sit on.

And it's not just the real royals who get fussy. Fictional ones are even worse. If I write "King Arthur," it looks majestic, legendary, almost holy. Write "king Arthur," and suddenly he's the guy who manages a comic book store. Then again, some of the royal titles I come across in my imagination are just begging to be demoted to lowercase. "duke of leftovers." "countess of cat hair." "prince of perpetual procrastination." Once you take away their capital crowns, they stop sounding regal and start sounding ridiculous. (Though, honestly, I'd still bow to the princess of procrastination—she'd understand me better than anyone.)

So, I've resigned myself to the fact that capital letters rule the royal court, whether I like it or not. They're the invisible crowns perched on the heads of words, and to leave them off is to risk literary scandal. Grammar may not have guillotines anymore, but I don't want to find out what happens to writers who *decapitalize* kings.

Yours obediently,
The Writer Who Bows Before Royal Pains

Entry 5: Brand Ego Trips

Dear Diary,

Today I spent half an hour arguing with a brand name. Not the company itself, just the written name. It was sitting in the middle of my sentence, smirking at me, daring me to capitalize it. The problem is, brands don't always play by the rules. They make up their own, and the rest of us are left pretending we totally meant to write it that way.

Take eBay. Lowercase "e," uppercase "B." What is that even about? Every time I type it, I feel like I'm in the middle of a ransom note assembled from mismatched magazine clippings. Or iPhone—a lowercase "i" followed by a capital "P." It looks like the word fell down a flight of stairs but got up again, determined to pretend it was intentional.

Brands, like some celebrities, love to test how much ego their spelling can get away with. k.d. lang, for instance, has made an entire career out of lowercase letters. Her name sits there, quietly refusing to stand up straight, like a student slouched in the back row of class. On the opposite end of the spectrum, you have companies like IKEA, which scream their names in all caps as if you'll forget them otherwise. Subtlety? Never heard of it.

The worst part is that style guides can't agree on how to handle these ego trips. Some say: respect the brand's choice. If they want to spell it "eBay," you honor the lowercase "e." Others say: forget it, you're the writer. Capitalize according to normal rules. So half the time I'm typing "eBay," and the other half I'm rebelling with "Ebay," secretly hoping no one notices.

But what happens when these names land at the beginning of a sentence or in a title? EBay doesn't want me to capitalize its precious "e," but English rules say otherwise. Do I really type "EBay Launches New Feature"? That looks like a typo wearing a business suit. And "Iphone"? The brand police would come knocking. Still, titles and sentence-openers force these lowercase rebels to stand up straight whether they like it or not.

It's chaos, Diary. And it's not just corporations. Musicians and authors have jumped on the bandwagon, too. Remember when will.i.am decided punctuation was part of his legal name? Or when Panic! at the Disco insisted on carrying that exclamation mark around like a hot potato? Imagine trying to read a history book where every other word has attitude issues. "The Treaty of Versailles, signed by Woodrow Wilson, David Lloyd George, Georges Clemenceau, and PANIC! AT THE DISCO." Not ideal.

But the truth is I always cave. I roll my eyes, but I follow the brand's lead. If Apple wants the "i" to crouch in lowercase while the "Phone" towers above, who am I to resist? If eBay wants to look like a typographical seesaw, fine. Because at the end of the day, it isn't really about grammar. It's about recognition. If I wrote "Ebay," some reader would write me an angry note saying, "Clearly you've never used the platform," as if a misplaced capital has erased my entire browsing history.

I sometimes fantasize about staging an intervention. Sitting brands down and saying, "Look, you're not fooling anyone. Lowercase doesn't make you cooler. Random capitals don't make you edgy." But, of course, they wouldn't listen. Brands live for attention, and weird capitalization is cheaper than a billboard.

So here I am, trapped in their ego trips, dutifully typing their names exactly the way they demand. Even if it makes me feel like I'm betraying everything I know about consistency.

Yours begrudgingly,
The Writer Who Keeps Giving In To Brand Ego

Entry 6: Geography Gone Wild

Dear Diary,

    I got lost in the wilderness of capitalization today. Not in the mountains themselves, but in the rules for naming them. Geography has decided it is far too important to follow a single set of guidelines. Rivers, mountains, valleys—each one wants to be capitalized, but only if the stars align just right.

    Take the Mississippi River. Capital "M," capital "R." Looks grand, majestic, like something carved into a monument. But if I write "the river in Mississippi," suddenly *river* slumps into lowercase while *Mississippi* keeps strutting around in its capital cloak. Same geography, different treatment. Apparently only the official, full names get the royal crown—the generic words have to slouch in lowercase.

    The same goes for mountains. *Mount Everest* gets the royal treatment, but take away its name and you're left with a plain old "mountain." Generic words don't get capital letters unless they're marching alongside their famous friends. Same with lakes: Lake Superior gets the spotlight, but strip away its title and it's just "a superior lake," lowercase and ordinary. Without the proper noun attached, the generic words are left scrubbing floors like Cinderella. Fancy ball? Capitals everywhere. Just hanging out? Back to lowercase rags.

    And then there are the compass points. I don't think I've ever been so confused. Capitalize *the South* when it refers to a region, but keep it lowercase when it's just a direction. "I'm traveling south" = humble lowercase. "I'm visiting the South" = capital letters, fried chicken, and cultural baggage. The rules say context matters, but context changes faster than weather in the Rockies.

    Of course, cities and countries are always capitalized—Paris, Canada, the Sahara Desert. But woe betide the poor writer who forgets to capitalize *Street* in "Baker Street" or *Avenue* in "Fifth Avenue." Those little location words are clingy. If they're part of the proper name, they demand a capital. If they're alone—"the street was dark"—they shrink back into lowercase as if nothing ever happened.

The whole thing makes me wonder who wrote these rules. Was there a secret council of cartographers somewhere, sipping tea and cackling over the confusion they'd cause? "Let's make north lowercase unless it means the North, and while we're at it, let's make sure rivers feel special only when fully introduced." Evil geniuses, the lot of them.

Sometimes I think we should just lowercase everything and call it a day. *the grand canyon. the pacific ocean. the rockies.* It would look casual, maybe even modern—like geography went minimalist. But lowercase "pacific ocean" doesn't exactly inspire awe, does it? It sounds less like a vast body of water and more like a neighborhood swimming pool.

So, I soldier on, memorizing the rules:

Names of specific places get capitals.
Generic descriptors do not.
Directions are lowercase unless they're regions.
And for the love of grammar, don't forget the "Street" in "Wall Street."

Geography may be wild, but it's not lawless. It just likes to keep me guessing, the way a trickster god might amuse itself by rearranging road signs. And I, poor mortal that I am, must follow the capitals wherever they lead—even if they lead me in circles.

Yours directionlessly,
The Writer Who Keeps Getting Lost in Capitals

Entry 7: Seasonal Affective Capitalization Disorder

Dear Diary,

I spent today arguing with the seasons. Not the weather—that would just be a waste of time. Spring, summer, fall, winter. They can't make up their minds about capitalization, and frankly, it's giving me whiplash.

Here's the deal: the seasons are lowercase most of the time. You write about *summer at the beach, winter dragging on forever,* or *fall making you trip over leaves and your own shoelaces.* But the moment you slap a season into the title of an event, it shows up in a tuxedo and demands a capital letter: *Winter Olympics, Summer Solstice, Spring Fling.* Suddenly these lowercase loafers are walking the red carpet like they own the place.

And that's the problem. The rules don't feel consistent—they feel like mood swings. The months get capitalized without question. *January, February, March.* Always dignified, always tall. But the poor seasons? Lowercase most of the time, unless they've been invited to the VIP section of the sentence. The months get to be proper nouns, while the seasons are treated like freeloaders crashing the party.

I once had a teacher who tried to explain it this way: "Think of the seasons as descriptions, not names. They describe the time of year, but they aren't unique enough to be capitalized—unless they're part of a unique title." Which makes sense in theory. But on the page? It just makes me second-guess every time I write "summer." Do I look lazy? Am I breaking a rule? Should I be apologizing to the sun?

What makes it worse is how emotional the seasons already are. *Spring* bursts in with allergies and optimism. *Summer* struts around in flip-flops, radiating smugness. *Fall* mopes about with pumpkin spice lattes, sighing dramatically. *Winter* sulks in the corner, draped in scarves. None of them need a reason to be moody, and yet the rules of capitalization have given them one.

I can't tell you how many times I've stared at a sentence and thought something like, *Maybe I'll just capitalize Winter this once. It looks nicer.* But then the guilt sets in. Style guides everywhere wag their fingers at me: lowercase unless it's part of a title. No exceptions. Meanwhile, "Spring" bats its eyes and begs me for to be capital. I am not strong enough to resist.

Sometimes I wish the seasons would unionize and demand equal treatment. If the months get capitals, why shouldn't they? Imagine the press conference: "We, the undersigned, Spring, Summer, Fall, and Winter, hereby demand the same typographical dignity as our cousins January through December, and Sunday through Monday." Honestly, I'd sign the petition.

Until then, I'll keep following the rules: lowercase for the everyday, capitals for the spotlight. It's summer vacation, but the Summer Olympics. A winter coat, but the Winter Games. The trick is remembering which events deserve capital letters and which ones are just Tuesday.

Yours in season,
The Writer Who Can't Stop Second-Guessing Summer

Entry 8: Days of Our Lives

Dear Diary,

I've discovered that time has a propensity for reminding us how important it is. While the ticking-clock kind of time tends to sneak by practically unnoticed, the calendar sort—the days, months, and holidays—they all insist on wearing capital letters like designer sunglasses, strutting around as if they're too important to mingle with the common nouns of the world. Monday isn't just a day; it proclaims that it's time to don our business casual attire and get back to work. If we spelled it "monday," we'd soon see PAST DUE pumping itself up. And no one wants that.

Months are no better. March barges in like it owns the season, April cries dramatically with all that rain, and December jingles into the room dragging a tree, a menorah, and an entire sleigh team behind it. Try writing "december" in lowercase and see if it doesn't look like you've ruined someone's childhood.

Holidays, of course, are the worst offenders. Christmas shows up overdressed every year, Easter hops around demanding pastel colors, and Halloween insists on being capitalized to match its all-caps scream of "BOO!" They know they'll get their capitals whether they deserve them or not. Even the quiet ones—like Arbor Day—get a shiny uppercase "A," as though the trees themselves would file a complaint if you left them out.

Meanwhile, words like "yesterday," "today," and "tomorrow" get no special treatment. They live in lowercase obscurity, doomed to stand in the shadows of Friday Night Plans. No one ever writes, "I can't wait for Tomorrow," unless they're quoting a show tune. Even then, it still looks like a typo.

What's worse is how inconsistent it all feels. We capitalize *New Year's Day* but not the hangover that follows. We capitalize *Valentine's Day* but not the box of regretful chocolates you bought for yourself on February fourteenth. Birthdays don't even make the cut—you can be the star of the party, but the word "birthday" is stuck slouching around in lowercase, as if it doesn't want anyone to know how old we really are.

It's a hierarchy, Diary. The days and months sit on their thrones of uppercase letters while ordinary words fight over crumbs. Try writing "sunday brunch" in lowercase, and suddenly it looks like a sad plate of cold eggs. Add the capital S, though—*Sunday brunch*—and suddenly it's champagne mimosas and overpriced avocado toast. Capitals change everything.

But the worst is when the days gang up on you in a planner or calendar. They march in military order— Sunday, Monday, Tuesday, Wednesday, Thursday, Friday, Saturday—like a filing cabinet you can't escape. You try to rebel, scribbling in lowercase, but the shame creeps in. Did you just disrespect Wednesday? No wonder it gives you a midweek crisis.

Months, on the other hand, wield emotional power. *August* feels like it's lounging on a beach chair, *October* smells faintly of pumpkin spice and turkey, and *January* stares at you with the cold, judgmental eyes of a gym membership you'll never use. Strip them of their capitals, and they collapse into something sad—"august" looks like a 90-pound weakling who just got sand kicked in his face.

Holidays are downright tyrannical. The capital letter isn't just grammar; it's branding. Write "christmas" in lowercase and someone will call you a Grinch. Write "independence day" without the capitals and you'll be accused of treason. Try spelling "halloween" with a lowercase h—ghosts will appear in your mirror to correct you.

So yes, time may be relentless, but it's also ridiculously vain. The calendar struts through our lives in capital letters, demanding attention, while lowercase words like "next week" or "last summer" are left sitting alone at the grammar lunch table. And we, obedient writers, just keep bowing down with our capital keys.

Yours chronologically,

DEAR DIARY; I'VE COMMITTED A CAPITAL OFFENSE 19

The Writer Who Keeps Bringing a Little Attitude to Holidays

Entry 9: Holy Caps, Batman!

Disclaimer: This entry isn't making fun of anyone's beliefs. It's only poking fun at the inconsistent capitalization rules around them. Please don't write me angry letters in ALL CAPS.

Dear Diary,

Religion and grammar should never mix, but try telling that to the alphabet. Divine beings have been demanding capitalization since the dawn of time, and the rules are about as consistent as a prophet's beard trimmer. God, with a capital G, clearly got the best PR contract in history. Write "god" in lowercase, and suddenly people accuse you of blasphemy, heresy, or at the very least, a typo. Capitalize "God," though, and it's like you've secured a backstage pass to Heaven.

Divine pronouns are the oddballs: some publishers capitalize **He**, **Him**, and **His** when referring to God; others keep them lowercase. Meanwhile, **I** is uppercase no matter where it shows up—because **I** is a special case of its own, but not because it outranks anyone in holiness. The result? A lot of pious pronoun dress-code drama.

Then there are the lowercase gods—plural. Greek gods, Roman gods, Norse gods, random neighborhood deities who like to lounge on cloud couches and meddle in human affairs. They get a lowercase **g** like it's some kind of demotion. Zeus, Hera, and Poseidon may have toppled empires, but they can't even land the uppercase G. Apparently, "gods" in general are just riffraff compared to the capitalized Big Guy. Imagine being Ares, god of war, and finding out you're linguistically beneath a pronoun. That's enough to start a Trojan War all over again.

And what about the rest of the pantheon? Ra, Odin, Vishnu—each one gets capitalized by name, but only because we're treating them like proper nouns, not because the grammar gods are feeling generous. Strip away the titles, and suddenly they're just lowercase divinities, slouching around like unemployed actors waiting for a casting call. "Excuse me, lowercase god reporting for duty—do you need a thunderstorm or a plague today?"

The chaos extends to holy books. The **Bible** is capitalized. The **Torah** is capitalized. The **Qur'an** is capitalized. But the word **bible** on its own doesn't always need a capital—if you're talking about *the Bible* as the sacred text, yes, capitalize it. But if you're using it generically ("a style bible," "a fisherman's bible," or "the hotel nightstand had a bible in the drawer"), lowercase is perfectly correct. And the word **scripture**? That one's vibe-based. Some houses prefer **Scripture** when they mean sacred writings collectively; others keep it lowercase unless it's part of a title. It's like the divine publishing industry has its own copy editors, and they're all using different style guides.

And let's not forget the random capitalizations people deploy when they want to sound profound. Writers get dramatic and suddenly **Love** is capitalized, **Fate** is capitalized, **Destiny** struts around like it's auditioning for a Broadway play. These words aren't gods, Diary. They're just nouns wearing dollar-store halos. No matter how many capitals you throw at **The Universe**, it's still not going to text you back.

Holidays join the holy confusion party, too. **Good Friday** and **All Saints' Day** walk around with their capital letters like sacred jewelry, while **Black Friday** tries to borrow the glow and becomes a stampede at the mall (house styles vary on capping that one in nonreligious contexts). Capitalization can make the difference between salvation and a clearance sale on air fryers.

Of course, the trickiest part is knowing when **not** to capitalize. Some folks cap every mention of **the Father, the Son,** or **the Holy Spirit**; others keep them lowercase and let context do the heavy lifting. Style guides disagree—one says reverential caps are optional and publisher-specific, another advises lowercase by default in general prose. The only way to stay sane is to pick a lane and be consistent.

And then there are people who capitalize **Heaven** but not **hell**. What is that about? I think it's because no one wants to give Hell too much attention. Either way, lowercase flames feel on-brand.

Bottom line, Diary: divinity has a complicated relationship with capital letters. When it comes to the Almighty, the sacred, or even the vaguely mystical, grammar keeps changing its hymnbook. Whether you're dealing with a lowercase pagan god, a capitalized pronoun in flowing robes, or a writer trying to remember if it's **Holy Spirit** or **holy spirit**, the smartest move is to choose a style and carry it through every page.

Yours reverently (but inconsistently),
The Writer Who Still Isn't Sure About "Holy Spirit"

Entry 10: Acronym Drama

Dear Diary,

I think acronyms are just letters that decided to unionize. They band together, march across the page, and demand to be read as if they're more important than regular words. Some strut around in all caps—**NASA**, **FBI**, **NATO**—like celebrities who refuse to take off their sunglasses indoors. Others mellow out, dropping into lowercase like they're trying to blend in with the crowd—*radar, scuba, laser*. They used to be big deals. Now they're just common nouns hanging out with the rest of us.

The drama lies in deciding which acronyms get to stay uppercase forever and which ones are forced into early retirement. **NASA** is still shouting, even though it was born in 1958. **SCUBA** (Self-Contained Underwater Breathing Apparatus) has been around longer, but it got tired of yelling and now prefers to nap in lowercase. It's not fair. How do space agencies get to keep their capital letters while divers lose theirs? It's almost like language is playing favorites.

Then there are the hybrids—things like **NaCl** or **pH**—half capitalized, half lowercase, and all attitude. They're like teenagers who can't decide if they want to obey the rules or slam the door in defiance. "Yes, Mother, I'll capitalize the N and the C, but I'm leaving the a and the i lowercase because I'm *expressing myself*." Acronyms aren't just words. They're angsty adolescents.

Not all acronyms are equal either. True acronyms are pronounceable: **NASA**, **UNICEF**, **OPEC**. Initialisms, on the other hand, require having each letter read (or said) individually, like **FBI** or **ATM**. Except sometimes acronyms pretend to be initialisms, and initialisms pretend to be acronyms, and suddenly I'm stuck wondering if I should be saying "N-A-S-D-A-Q" or "Nasdaq." It's like a masquerade ball for capital letters, and everyone's swapping masks halfway through the dance.

Of course, acronyms also love to create confusion. **ATM machine**? That's like saying Automatic Teller Machine machine. **PIN number**?

Personal Identification Number number. **VIN number?** Vehicle Identification Number number. Redundancy is their favorite party trick. They sneak in, repeat themselves, and no one notices because they're too dazzled by the capitals.

Some impostors sneak into the acronym party, too. **IKEA** looks like an acronym, but it's really Ingvar Kamprad's clever way of hiding his name (plus his farm and hometown) inside a furniture empire. **LEGO** isn't technically an acronym either—it's a mashup of two Danish words, *leg godt* ("play well"). But because they swagger around in all caps, they get mistaken for acronyms all the time. The alphabet soup crowd doesn't seem to mind; the more letters at the party, the merrier.

Texting has introduced us to a wide variety of acronyms and initialisms. **LOL, OMG, BRB**—they're basically shorthand hieroglyphics. Some even try to soften their tone by slipping into lowercase—*lol, brb, idk*. Lowercase makes it sound like you're whispering, while ALL CAPS makes it sound like you're laughing so hard you might pee your pants. Tone, apparently, is a matter of capitalization.

People like to invent their own. Acronyms are addictive. I came up with these ones off the top of my head:

D.A.R.N. — *Diaries Against Random Nonsense*. Membership: you and me.

C.A.P.S. — *Capitals Are Pretty Stubborn*. Motto: "We will not be lowercased."

See? Instant authority. Slap some dots between the letters, and suddenly it feels official.

The truth is that acronyms are just shortcuts that can make life easier sometimes. Some might scream in all caps forever. Some will quietly fade into lowercase. Some are sketchy chemistry experiments. And the rest? They sneak into our texts and emails, pretending they're helping when they're really just making everything sound like a secret code.

DEAR DIARY; I'VE COMMITTED A CAPITAL OFFENSE

Yours A.C.R.O.N.Y.M.I.C.A.L.L.Y. (Always Creating Ridiculous Outbursts, Nurturing Your Manuscripts In Capitalization And Laughing Loudly, Yes),

The Writer Who Suffers From Capital Confusion

Entry 11: The Capital of Creativity

Dear Diary,

Some writers collect fountain pens. Others collect rejection letters. Me? I think we all secretly collect capital letters—and then fling them at abstract concepts like confetti. The result? *Love, Fate, Destiny, The Darkness.* Capitalized, they stomp onto the page in heavy boots, demanding respect they rarely deserve.

It starts innocently enough. You're writing about love—ordinary, lowercase love—and suddenly you feel like it isn't carrying enough weight. So you capitalize it. *Love.* Now it's not just a feeling; it's a character. It has agency, attitude, maybe even a Netflix deal. And if you're a teenager scribbling in an actual diary (no offense, Diary), suddenly *Love* is the villain who ruined your Friday night.

Writers throughout history have leaned hard on this trick. Poets especially. They can't just write about fate—they must write about *Fate*, with a capital F, as though destiny were a stern aunt tapping her foot in the corner. Same goes for *Death.* Lowercase death is inevitable but manageable. *Death*—capitalized—is a cloaked figure waiting at the bus stop, probably with exact change.

Then there's *The Darkness.* Why do writers keep capitalizing that one? Lowercase darkness is just... the absence of light. Bump into a coffee table, stub your toe, mutter a curse. But *The Darkness*? That's a Marvel villain, a heavy-metal band, or the reason Chad broke up with you in tenth grade.

This is where creativity turns melodramatic. A capitalized concept looks Important, but when too many of them show up on the page, the prose starts to look like it's wearing too much eyeliner. "She was trapped by *Fear*, tempted by *Desire*, and haunted by *The Past.*" That's not literature—it's a Hot Topic clearance rack.

Of course, sometimes it works. Religious texts use capital letters for reverence: *Truth, Light, Word.* Political speeches do it too: *Freedom,*

DEAR DIARY; I'VE COMMITTED A CAPITAL OFFENSE

Justice, Democracy. It's not wrong—it's rhetoric. Capitalization can lend gravity. It can elevate an idea. But overdo it, and you're not elevating—you're just inflating.

Modern marketing has stolen the trick and turned it into a business plan. Ads capitalize random words to make them sound magical: "Join the Movement." "Feel the Power." "Experience the Magic." Nobody ever invites you to join *the movement* in lowercase—it sounds like a trip to the bathroom.

And let's not forget personal journals. Not you, Diary—you're wonderful. I mean the kind teenagers keep under their mattresses. Every entry brims with capitalized emotions: *Hate, Pain, Longing*. Sometimes whole relationships are reduced to capitalized archetypes: *The Boy, The Crush, The Betrayal.* Lowercase is apparently too casual for heartbreak.

The problem is, these capitalized concepts don't age well. What felt profound in the moment ends up reading like melodrama in hindsight. Ten years later, you dig out that old notebook and groan, "Did I really write about *The End of Everything* just because someone didn't text me back?" Yes. Yes, you did.

But maybe that's the charm. Capitals can make us look ridiculous, but they also capture the intensity of how we felt in the moment. Sometimes writers need a big, flashy *Love* or *Destiny* to pin down the chaos in their characters' lives. Grammar purists may scoff, but creativity is supposed to be a little messy.

Still, I think I'll try to use my capital letters sparingly. I'll save them for occasions when I want to sound profound, not petulant. And if *The Darkness* really is out there, I hope it has the decency to bring snacks.

Yours melodramatically,
The Writer Who Once Capitalized The Darkness and Regrets Nothing

Entry 12: Family Feud

Dear Diary,

Today I learned that capitalizing family relationships is... Well, relative!

Take Mom. If I write "I love my mom," she's lowercase, casual, humble, probably baking an apple pie for dessert. But the moment I drop the "my," she commands my respect: "I love Mom." Here, she enters the page in high heels, daring anyone to question her. Same woman, same relationship, but suddenly her own person.

It's the same with Dad, Aunt Sue, Cousin Larry, and all the rest. Used as names, they must be capitalized. But the second you get a little possessive, down they go. "my dad," "her aunt," "our cousin." Apparently, adding a pronoun is enough to knock them right off the throne.

The inconsistency drives me nuts. "Uncle Bob took us fishing" looks respectable, like a Norman Rockwell painting. "My uncle Bob took us fishing" looks like Bob just wandered out of lowercase purgatory. And heaven forbid I leave out his name altogether—"my uncle took us fishing"—suddenly he's been tossed into oblivion. Poor guy. No wonder he drinks.

Grandparents are no better. "Grandma" with a capital is everyone's sweet sweater-knitting matriarch. Whereas, "my grandma" is just some random woman in slippers who might or might not slip you a fiver. Same genetic material, wildly different vibes.

Nicknames are a whole separate brawl. "Big Brother" gets a capital if it's Orwell or a reality show. But "my big brother" sulks around in lowercase. Same with "the twins." Capitalize it, and they become a terrifying urban legend. Lowercase, and they're just two kids fighting over a juice box.

I can't forget the in-laws. Do I write "Mother-in-Law" as though she's a Marvel villain, or "my mother-in-law," which is only slightly ominous? If I get it wrong, am I making a grammar mistake or starting a family war? Hard to say. No one ever says, "Mother-in-Law, please pass the potatoes." unless they're a character in a Victorian penny dreadful, so it's probably safe to stick to lowercase and talk about her instead of to her.

I once wrote "Happy birthday, dad" in a card, and he circled it in red like an English teacher. "Dad" deserves a capital, he said, especially when you're talking directly to him. Apparently, lowercase was a sign of disrespect. Which raises the question: if I had written "Happy birthday, dictator," would that have been more or less insulting?

The truth is, Diary, the rules make sense—in theory. Capitalize family titles when they stand in for a name. Keep them lowercase when they're general descriptors. But in practice, every sentence feels like a grammar minefield, with relatives waiting to pounce on the slightest demotion.

So here's my plan: I'll capitalize Mom, Dad, Grandma, Grandpa, Aunt, and Uncle when I'm using them as names, and leave them lowercase when I'm not. And if my relatives complain, I'll tell them to take it up with the Chicago Manual of Style. Because let's be honest: if anyone can survive a family feud, it's Chicago.

Yours genealogically,
The Writer Who Accidentally Demoted Mom

Entry 13: Academic Inflations

Dear Diary,

 Today I discovered that degrees and institutions are just as needy as relatives when it comes to capitalization. Honestly, they might be worse. At least Mom only wants a capital letter when she's standing in for her own name. Universities? They want the whole sentence to bow down.

 Take degrees. If I write "She earned a master's degree," that's lowercase, simple, perfectly correct. But the moment I specify the field of study, those capital letters demand attention: "Master of Arts in English." It's like the degree insists, *Don't just say I'm a degree—say exactly which degree I am, with full regalia, please.* Bachelor of Science, Doctor of Philosophy, Master of Fine Arts... They're less academic honors than parade floats rolling by in caps and gowns.

 But here's the kicker: strip away the specifics and they go right back to lowercase. "She earned her doctorate." "He finished his bachelor's degree." It's the academic equivalent of Clark Kent putting on glasses—one second, superhero; the next, just a guy standing next to a phone booth.

 Institutions are no better. Capitalize the full, proper name—"University of Chicago," "Harvard University," "Hogwarts School of Witchcraft and Wizardry"—and suddenly they loom large, casting long shadows across the page. But say "the university," and poof! Lowercase, humble, invisible. Same campus, same tuition fees, zero prestige.

 I could go on and on about "College," but I won't do that. "She's in college" is lowercase, casual, like she's just hanging out between classes. But slap on the full title "College of Arts and Sciences"—and suddenly it's marching across the page with brass instruments.

 The inconsistency makes me suspicious. Are capital letters really about grammar here, or are they about ego? Universities love their capitals the way professors love footnotes: excessively. Write "the school" in lowercase and it sounds like a normal place where you might learn something. Write "The School" and suddenly you're in a cult initiation ceremony.

And then there's alumni bragging. "He went to the University of Toronto"—capitalized, crisp, formal. "He went to university in Toronto"—lowercase, vague, like maybe he just hung around the campus bookstore for four years. The difference between capital and lowercase is the difference between "I have a diploma" and "I have some very expensive souvenirs."

The rules are simple: capitalize full, official names of degrees and institutions, but keep it lowercase when you're speaking generally. But in practice? Every commencement program reads like it was typeset by a capitalization cult.

Yours pedantically,
The Writer Who Survived Higher Education but Not Its Capitals

Capital Crimes Report

Dear Diary,

    This is it. The trial is over, the verdict is in, and I stand guilty on all counts of capitalization misconduct. I've committed every crime in the book—and now I must face the consequences. The charges are as follows:

    Count One: Excessive Reverence. Guilty. I once capitalized *Love*, *Fate*, and *Destiny* in the same paragraph, as though they were a holy trinity of melodrama. My only defense is that I was feeling poetic at the time. The court was not moved.

    Count Two: Unlawful Shouting in ALL CAPS. Guilty. I've sent text messages that read like emergency broadcasts: *"WHERE ARE YOU???"* Lowercase was available, but I chose violence.

    Count Three: Title Case Abuse. Guilty. I confess to writing a headline that capitalized every single word, including "of," "to," and "in." It was Capital Letter Soup, and it still haunts me at night.

    Count Four: Reckless Lowercasing. Guilty. I once typed "september" in a professional email. September deserved better from me.

    Count Five: Redundancy with Acronyms. Guilty. "PIN number." Enough said.

    Count Six: Personification of Abstract Concepts. Guilty. I gave *The Darkness* its own monologue. Honestly, Diary, I'd do it again.

    The jury of style guides was not sympathetic. Chicago frowned, AP shook its head, MLA refused to make eye contact, and APA just handed me a citation form. Sentence: life in grammar purgatory, with no chance of parole until I learn to keep my capitals in check.

    But as I sit here reflecting on my crimes, I realize something: maybe capital letters aren't villains after all. Maybe they're just unruly characters in a story we've been telling for centuries. They can shout, yes. They can strut, yes. But they can also clarify, or elevate our writing. Without them, *god* and *God* would mean the same thing, *us* and *U.S.* would be indistinguishable, and we might end up bringing our passport to Thanksgiving dinner by mistake.

So perhaps my punishment isn't really a punishment; it's awareness. From now on, when I reach for a capital letter, I'll think twice. Do I need it? Does it earn its place? Or am I just giving *Chocolate Cake* more importance than it deserves? (Trick question. Chocolate Cake always deserves importance.)

In the end, Diary, I don't regret my capital crimes. They've taught me that grammar isn't just about rules—it's about choices. Every uppercase letter is a decision, a splash of emphasis, a little drama on the page. And maybe that's why we love them, even when they're loud, bossy, and inconsistent.

Case closed.

Yours Sentenced Fairly,

The Repeat Offender in Title Case

Glossary of Capital Confusion

This glossary is here to clear up the jargon and shine a spotlight on the quirks of capitalization. Some entries are serious, some are snarky, all are designed to keep you in the know.

ALL CAPS

When letters stop speaking and start screaming. Useful for acronyms, emergency alerts, and making sure your Facebook rant gets you unfriended.

Acronym

A group of capital letters pretending to be a real word (NASA, SCUBA). Some stay fancy forever; others eventually slouch into lowercase like exhausted celebrities.

CamelCase

When words are SmashedTogetherWithoutSpaces and random Capitals pop up like speed bumps. Beloved by tech companies and people who think their startup looks cooler without spaces.

Capital Letter

The big sibling of the alphabet. Shows up at the start of sentences, in names, and anytime someone wants to look Important. Often bossy.

Capitalization

The practice of deciding which words get VIP treatment with tall hats (aka capital letters). Sometimes it marks beginnings (sentences, names, titles). Sometimes it's a matter of style (the Great Debate over Chocolate Cake vs. chocolate cake). Always a power move in the orthography world.

Initialism

An acronym's quieter cousin. You say and read it letter by letter—FBI, ATM, DIY. Rarely pronounceable, unless you're trying to invent new sounds.

Internet/internet

A capitalization debate that lasted longer than most celebrity marriages. Once proudly capitalized (*The Internet*), it has now mostly been demoted to lowercase (*internet*), except in places where editors still haven't gotten the memo.

Lowercase
The introverts of the alphabet. They do most of the work but rarely get the glory. Stylish in minimalism, also favored by teenagers in text messages.

Orthography
A very serious word for the not-so-serious business of spelling, capitalization, and punctuation. Basically the dress code of writing: which letters wear which outfits, and whether anyone remembered to put on matching shoes.

Proper Noun
A noun so full of itself it demands a capital: *Paris, Coca-Cola, Mississippi River*. You may be a river, but you'll never be *The* River.

Redundancy (Acronym Edition)
When people write "PIN number" or "ATM machine." Basically, Capitalized Letters Having an Identity Crisis.

Reverential Caps
Capital letters used for divine or sacred words: *God, Him, Holy Spirit*. Depending on your style guide, these are either optional, or a lightning strike waiting to happen.

Sentence case
The chill headline style. Only the first word and proper nouns get a capital. Reads like your friend casually spilling gossip over brunch.

Small Caps
Uppercase letters that accidentally went through the dryer and came out half a size smaller—yet still insist on attending the opera in full formal attire. Used in book design, legal contracts, or by people who want acronyms to feel extra fancy. *Example: A novel might open a chapter*

with "**Once Upon A Time** there was a dragon" set in small caps for that extra touch of drama.

Style Guide

The grammar referee that makes the rules. Unfortunately, no two style guides agree on anything. CMoS says one thing, AP another, MLA sulks in the corner, and APA cites you for everything.

The Darkness

An ordinary absence of light until you capitalize it. Then it becomes a villain, a band, or a phase in your high school poetry.

Title Case

The formal headline style. Every Important Word Stands Tall, except the poor little articles and prepositions, which are forced to crouch in lowercase. Unless, of course, a style guide decides otherwise.

Word Inflation

The habit of capitalizing concepts (*Love*, *Destiny*, *Fate*) to make them seem bigger than they are. Works until you start doing it for *Chocolate Cake* and *Laundry*.

YOLO Caps

Random Capitals thrown into sentences because Why Not. Often seen in government memos, junk mail, and social media rants. Not endorsed by any sane editor.

It's Time to Play... Cap or No Cap?

Welcome to everyone's favorite grammar game show, where the prizes are bragging rights and the loser faces eternal shame in front of their editor. The rules are simple: decide which of the following examples have been capitalized correctly.

Round One: Seasonal Shenanigans

1. I love summer.
2. I love Summer.

Round Two: Relative Chaos

1. My mom is coming over for dinner.
2. I told Mom to bring dessert.

Round Three: Holiday Hazards

1. We always go sledding on christmas.
2. We always go sledding on Christmas.

Round Four: Geographic Guesswork

1. I climbed mount Everest.
2. I climbed Mount Everest.

Round Five: Sacred or Secular?

1. I read a bible in the hotel room.
2. I read the Bible in the hotel room.

Round Six: Headline Hijinks

1. Local man rescues duck from pond
2. Local Man Rescues Duck From Pond

Round Seven: Direction Dilemmas

1. We drove west until the road ended.
2. We drove West until the road ended.

Round Eight: Academic Attire

1. I finally earned my master's degree.
2. I finally earned my Master's Degree.

Round Nine: Marketing Madness

1. Experience the Magic of Laundry Detergent.
2. Experience the magic of laundry detergent.

Round Ten: Abstract Overload

1. She believed in truth, beauty, and justice.
2. She believed in Truth, Beauty, and Justice.

Round Eleven: Job Title Jitters

1. My mom works as a senator.
2. My mom works as a Senator.

Round Twelve: Destiny or drama?

1. It was her fate to marry a dentist.
2. It was her Fate to marry a dentist.

If you aced it, congratulations—you win bragging rights, a shiny imaginary trophy, and the ability to correct your friends at dinner parties (whether they like it or not). If you struggled, don't worry—you're still leaving with the consolation prize: a deeper appreciation for just how ridiculous capitalization rules can be.

And a copy of this book!

Cap or No Cap? Answer Key

Round One: *summer* lowercase (unless it's part of a title). "Summer" with a capital is just showing off.

Round Two: Both are right — lowercase when it's generic, uppercase when it's used as a name. Think of "Mom" as a proper noun when it's standing alone.

Round Three: Christmas demands a capital — the baby Jesus and Santa Claus both insist.

Round Four: Proper nouns like "Mount Everest" always get capitals. Lowercase and you're just hiking a generic hill.

Round Five: Both work, but mean different things. Lowercase = a generic "bible" of knowledge. Uppercase = the sacred text. Context is king.

Round Six: Both are acceptable depending on style. AP likes Sentence case (1), Chicago prefers Title Case (2). The duck is happy either way.

Round Seven: Lowercase for directions (west), uppercase only if it's a proper place (the West, the Midwest).

Round Eight: Lowercase unless you're naming the full degree title (Master of Arts, Master of Science). Otherwise, humble it down.

Round Nine: Option 2 is technically correct, but ads love to sprinkle capitals like glitter at a kid's birthday party. Proceed with caution

Round Ten: Lowercase is standard; uppercase is dramatic emphasis. Capitalizing all three makes it sound like you're writing for a superhero movie.

Round Eleven: Lowercase unless you're using it as a formal title before a name (*Senator Smith*). Otherwise, keep it humble.

Round Twelve: Lowercase for everyday destiny, uppercase if you're auditioning for a Greek tragedy.

A Sneak Peek at What's to Come

If you thought capital letters were unruly, just wait until words themselves start misbehaving. Half the time, they don't even mean what we think they mean. Malapropisms, misuses, and phrases that have gone completely off the rail are the linguistic equivalent of wearing socks with sandals and insisting it's a fashion statement.

The next installment of the Dear Diary Style Files, ***Dear Diary; I Don't Think That Word Means What I Think It Means***, takes aim at words and phrases that trip us up, embarrass us, and occasionally turn our writing into comedy sketches. From "literally" to "moot point" to words that sound much smarter than they are.

What follows is a sneak peek at the everyday word crimes we've all committed, complete with diary-level confessions and just enough sass to make a dictionary blush.

Entry 1: Literally the Worst

Dear Diary,

"Literally" has trust issues. It was designed to mean *exactly what it says*—no exaggeration, no wiggle room. But now? It's the word people drag along to every overblown claim. "I literally died laughing." "My brain literally exploded." Unless the obituary section has resorted to stand-up comedy, that never happened.

The poor word is exhausted. It started life as a sturdy little adverb meaning "in a literal sense, <u>without metaphor</u>." You could count on it to keep things grounded. But over time, writers started getting cheeky. By the 1700s, even respectable authors were using it for emphasis. Jane Austen did it. Charles Dickens did it. F. Scott Fitzgerald dropped a hyperbolic "literally" into *The Great Gatsby*. It's oddly comforting to know that when I complain about reality stars misusing it, I'm also shaking my fist at Dickens.

The trouble is, once dictionaries noticed this "figurative literally" sneaking around, they had a choice: wag their fingers and scold, or shrug and make it official. Guess which one they chose? Yep. Most dictionaries now list both meanings: the precise one, and the exaggerated one. Which means, Diary, that "literally" now officially means its opposite. I can't decide if that's linguistic evolution or the literary version of Stockholm syndrome.

What makes it worse is how casually people drop it into conversation. "I literally can't even." Do I call an ambulance? Or do I just hand them a snack and assume they mean "I'm mildly inconvenienced"? "I was literally glued to my seat." Really? Did the fire department have to come with solvent? "My boss literally bit my head off." In that case, I'd like to see the police report.

The sad part is, sometimes I almost do it myself. I'll be typing along and write "I literally cried" when I mean "I moaned a little." And then my editor brain slams on the brakes. Backspace, backspace. I can't let

DEAR DIARY; I'VE COMMITTED A CAPITAL OFFENSE

"literally" get away with exaggeration—it's like letting a toddler drive a car. Just because it *wants* to do something doesn't mean it should.

Of course, the language nerd in me knows that words shift meaning over time. "Awful" used to mean "awe-inspiring." "Nice" once meant "ignorant." "Egregious" used to be a compliment. Maybe "literally" is just going through its rebellious teenage years. But does it really need to turn into a double agent? Having a word mean one thing and its opposite is chaos, Diary. Pure chaos.

And then there's pop culture. Every sitcom character seems to sprinkle "literally" into their lines like it's parsley. Reality stars shout it across kitchens. Politicians pepper it into speeches. It's become filler, emphasis, drama—everything except what it was actually meant to be. Somewhere, the original definition is quietly weeping into its Oxford English Dictionary entry.

The truth is, "literally" is almost never necessary. If you say "I laughed until I cried," that's vivid enough. If you say "My brain exploded," people know it's a metaphor. We get it. And if you ever do find yourself in a situation where "literally" is required — like "I literally stepped on a Lego"—then, by all means, use it. You've earned it.

So yes, "literally" has become the poster child for misused words. I wish I could stage an intervention, hand it a blanket, and tell it to take a nap. But until then, every time I hear someone say "I literally can't live without my morning latte," I will quietly wish them good luck surviving the zombie apocalypse.

Yours exasperatedly,
The Writer Who Is Figuratively Dead Inside

Entry 2: Moot Point vs. Mute Point

Dear Diary,

Today I stumbled across the phrase "mute point." Mute. As in silent. As in "this argument has lost its voice and will now be communicated via interpretive dance." I shouldn't laugh, but I do. A "mute point" sounds less like a debate and more like two people glaring at each other across a table in total silence.

The phrase people usually want is "moot point." That's the original, borrowed from legal jargon. Back in the day, a "moot" was a meeting where lawyers-in-training argued hypothetical cases—debates with no real consequence. Over time, "moot point" came to mean "irrelevant" or "academic." But somewhere along the way, ears got confused, and "moot" slipped quietly into "mute."

And honestly? I get it. "Moot" isn't a word we toss around much outside this one phrase. "Mute," on the other hand, shows up on TV remotes. People know mute. They don't know moot. So, when the brain has to choose between a dusty courtroom term and a button you press to shut up the commercials, it picks the button every time.

Of course, once you picture it literally, it gets ridiculous. "That's a mute point" conjures an image of a lawyer standing up in court, opening his mouth, and nothing coming out. Or two philosophers sitting across from each other, both holding up signs that read, "I disagree, but quietly." The whole debate is just one long awkward pause.

So, here's the rule I intend to follow: it's "moot point" if I mean irrelevant, debatable, or academic. "Mute point" is just a typo in a Halloween costume. I might use it if I want to be funny—otherwise, I'll make my point loud and clear.

Yours audibly,
The Writer Who Will Not Be Silenced

Entry 3: Me, Myself, and I (And My Confusion)

Dear Diary,

Sometimes I think pronouns are just out to mess with me. Especially *me, myself,* and *I*. They're like a dysfunctional trio of siblings who can't stop fighting in the back seat of the grammar car. "He and I went to the store." "He and me went to the store." "He and myself went to the store." Somewhere, an English teacher is weeping over her red pen.

Let's start with *I*. It's the golden child—the subject pronoun. *I went to the store.* Simple, straightforward. But throw another person into the sentence and suddenly things get dicey. "He and I went to the store" is fine, but people panic and swap *I* for *me*. Why? Because *me* feels friendlier, less formal, more natural. Unfortunately, it's also wrong in that context.

Then there's poor *me*. It's supposed to be the object—the one things happen to. *He gave the book to me.* Perfectly normal. But when people try to sound fancy, they overcorrect. "He gave the book to I." I! As if they've knighted themselves mid-sentence. "Sir I, Defender of Incorrect Grammar."

And then comes *myself,* the troublemaker. It's meant for two jobs: reflexive (*I hurt myself*) or emphatic (*I baked the cake myself*). But somewhere along the way, *myself* decided it wanted a bigger career. Now it barges into sentences uninvited: "He gave the book to myself." No, he did not. *Myself* is not a substitute for *me*. It's not a fancier version. It's just confused.

The funniest part is how many professionals—politicians, CEOs, newscasters—fall into the trap. "Please contact John or myself if you have questions." They think it sounds polished. Really it sounds like John and *myself* don't know what we're talking about.

I get it, though. *I* feels too stiff. *Me* feels too casual. *Myself* feels like a safe middle ground. But grammar isn't about feelings; it's about function.

And function says: *I* is for subjects, *me* is for objects, and *myself* is for when you're doing something to yourself.

Still, I catch myself hesitating sometimes. I'll type "between you and I" and then hear the ghosts of every English teacher I've ever had shrieking in unison. Backspace, backspace. It's "between you and me." Every. Single. Time.

I know I don't always get it right on the first try either. These three pronouns are sneaky. They show up at odd hours, switch places, and whisper bad advice. But when I finally untangle them and get it right, I feel like I deserve a medal. Or at least a slice of cake. That I baked myself.

Yours reflectively,

The Writer Who Keeps Fighting with Herself

Also by Saoirse Temple

Bounders
The Fire of Orhowyn
The Amber Chalice

Dear Diary Style Files
Dear Diary: Punctuation Can't Save the World (But It Did Save Grandma)
Dear Diary: I Have 99 Problems and All of Them Are Numbers
Dear Diary: I Think the Alphabet is Gaslighting Me!
Dear Diary; I've Committed a Capital Offense

Watch for more at https://www.saoirsetemple.com/.

About the Author

Saoirse Temple is a professional editor and book coach who specializes in helping indie authors make their dream of being published come true. A long-time advocate of self-publishing, Saoirse enjoys sharing in the success of authors of all types of works. When she isn't editing or writing, she spends her time knitting, cross stitching, and exploring Grande Prairie, where she makes her home. Follow Saoirse on Facebook: www.facebook.com/saoirsetempleediting Patreon: www.patreon.com/SaoirseTemple Instagram: @saoirsealt

Read more at www.saoirsetemple.com.

www.ingramcontent.com/pod-product-compliance
Lightning Source LLC
Chambersburg PA
CBHW031433040426
42444CB00006B/786